"*The Starlight She Becomes* is a beautiful collection of transformation and acceptance. Parker's words are drenched with honesty and care. A much needed celebration of being trans and reminder of what we're fighting for and how worth the fight it is. This book made me want to grab a coffee with Parker and give her a hug."
— MICHAELA ANGEMEER
author of *Please Look into the Mirror*
"A beautifully vulnerable metamorphosis, Parker Lee masterfully guides us through her most authentic work to date."
— ALEX AND
author of *Between Scyl*
"A celestial journey that w
galaxies of self-discovery,
sapphic romance. Parker Lee has become an expert at balancing beauty with brutal honesty, & she has once again proven herself to be an essential voice of the millennial generation."
— AMANDA LOVELACE
author of *she followed the moon back to herself*
T0405908

The Starlight She Becomes

Poems

Parker Lee

the starlight she becomes contains sensitive material
relating to the following topics:

anxiety and depression, alcohol abuse, death, disordered eating, gender dysphoria, queerphobia, the covid-19 pandemic, passive suicidal ideation, and potentially more.

Please remember to practice self-care before, during, and after reading.

Published by Central Avenue Poetry, an imprint of Central Avenue Marketing Ltd.
centralavenuepublishing.com

the starlight she becomes

Trade Paperback: 978-1-77168-414-9
Epub: 978-1-77168-415-6

Published in Canada
Printed in United States of America

1. POETRY / LGBT 2. POETRY / Themes & Subjects - Inspiration

1 3 5 7 9 10 8 6 4 2

for

every version

of myself

that has ever

and will ever

exist.

Dear Reader,

This book has probably been the most difficult one for me to write thus far. After I turned in the manuscript for my book *coffee days whiskey nights* in January of 2020, I immediately began working on the next one. Up until that point, I had been consistent in releasing at least one book a year, and I had no intention of breaking that trend, but I found myself very lost as to what I wanted this book to become. A few months later, the COVID-19 pandemic hit, and needless to say, it didn't make writing any easier.

I think it goes without saying that the pandemic changed all of us collectively, and this book is a direct result of the transformation I went through over the last four, nearly five years. With that said, it's important to note that while this book does contain poems that directly reference the pandemic, I didn't want this to be a book about the pandemic. Instead, it's a book about not just surviving, but thriving. It's a book about overcoming and becoming. And it's a book about trans joy and sapphic love.

Thank you so much for reading, and for coming on this journey with me.

With love and starlight,

Parker

Contents

MOONRISE

SUNRISE

STARDUST

MOONRISE

it's me, but better

it's 6:00 am
and i am up before the sun.
i've rebranded myself
a morning person, you see.
i even have a routine now:

wake up
make coffee
do yoga
meditate
write

that's where i always get stuck.
i'm in a better place now,
and inspiration isn't always easy
to come by when you've stopped
being your own worst enemy.

i think about reopening the scars
i have from the last time i bled
myself dry in the name of "art,"
but that's not me anymore.

no more resurrecting the past
and giving it new life on paper.
what's dead will remain buried,
while i focus on *living* for a change.

don't call it an exorcism

it feels good to finally be in control
of my own life again. i've been on autopilot

for two years while my demons took my body
out on a road trip through every city my issues

call home. at least, that's the metaphor i would've
used had i not done so much work on myself.

because as hard as it is to admit, that self-destructive
being isn't some otherworldly entity pulling my strings,

but a living, breathing part of who i am at my core.
i needed to understand that before i could ever think

of coming back to myself. i needed to acknowledge
my shadow instead of pretending it doesn't exist.

i needed to understand it to understand myself.
i needed to learn how to walk side by side with it,

because try as you might, there's no outrunning
the very thing that lives inside of you.

pocket-sized rebellion

i once wrote about how i wouldn't put myself in a box to meet another's expectations, but all i've done is taken myself out of a metaphorical box and put myself into a digital one, curating myself like an influencer's social media feed. branding myself for double-taps to beat an algorithm that casts judgement as harshly as any human, breaking myself down into bytesized pieces to make my highly-debated trans existence more digestible for everyone. but i'm so much more than can be confined to a 1080 x 1080 square, so i'm taking a step back and giving myself permission to do exactly what i've spent the last three years preaching about:

simply *be.*

magnum opus

sometimes i wonder if anyone would miss me
if i just disappeared. deleted all of my social media
accounts and ran off to live in the woods. i wonder
if i unplugged myself from reality and let the poems
i've written exist in my place, if i let my art be my legacy,
would that be enough for me? if my last poem is my last
poem, would i be content with my final words? at one point,
i might've said yes, but now, i'm not so sure i've even written
my best line, let alone my best poem. in 2018, i thought
i had completed my *magnum opus*, but now i ask myself—
can your *great work* be your *great work* if nobody sees it?

better help yourself first

i subscribe to an online counseling app because it's cheaper than seeing a therapist in person and if i'm being honest, i've never been good at speaking my truth out loud without liquor in my veins or a poetry book in my hands. i pour myself into the chatbox like i poured bottles down the drain the last time i said i was breaking up with whiskey. i tell her about my binge eating and drinking tendencies. i tell her about my body image issues. i tell her about my passive suicidal ideation. i tell her about my gender dysphoria and how i think it's the root of ~~all~~ most of my problems. i tell her about how i've been fixated on the idea of medically transitioning even though sober me refuses to admit that it's the answer to the unasked question. when she affirms me, i am one hundred percent certain that i one hundred percent wanted to be talked out of myself. so i go without checking in for a week, and when i finally do, i tell my counselor that i am doing better, and that is not a lie, but it isn't the truth, either. another week goes by and i tell her i'll be cancelling my subscription to the app before it renews. i thank her for all of her help, and that *is* the truth, because she did help me, even if i wasn't yet ready to help myself.

I KNOW WHAT'S BEST FOR ME
BUT I'M TOO AFRAID
TO LET MYSELF HAVE IT.

astral

i sit cross-legged
eyes closed
body planted
like a tree
roots growing
connecting me
to the earth
inhale
exhale
imagine sunlight
pouring
into me
from the top
down
inhale
exhale
imagine myself
growing
beyond
my body
beyond
the room
beyond
my home
beyond
borough limits
beyond
state lines
beyond
borders
inhale

exhale
imagine my soul
untethered
from the body
soaring
through
blue skies
through
the atmosphere
through
the galaxy
amongst
the stars
inhale
exhale
return to
my body
my mind
inhale
exhale
slowly
open eyes.

bizarro world

it's early march 2020—
i step into an airplane in detroit
and step out into a time capsule
just as the locks click shut.

schools: closed
parks: closed
coffee shops: closed
liquor stores: ~~closed~~ open

if this is the end of
the world as we know it,
then let us drink until
the sun burns out.

the best i've ever been

i'm in such a good place
these days you wouldn't believe it.

sure, i've started drinking again,
but i'm practicing the art of moderation now.

sure, i've started counting calories again,
but i'm being so much more flexible with my goals.

sure, i'm exercising every single day again,
but i've made it a lifestyle now, not a punishment.

sure, my gender dysphoria is haunting me again,
but it isn't as bad as it was a few months ago.

i'm in such a good place
these days, and if i weren't always

trying to convince myself of that,
i wouldn't believe it either.

groundhog day

the days bleed together,
a year swallowed quicker
than the shot of bourbon
you gulp down after claiming
you're done for the night—
all burn and none of the escape.
it's like time is running out
and that there's too much of it
all at once, and i keep
lapsing. i keep falling back
into my old ways, because
what is the point in trying to change
when nothing ever changes?
i count the days like calories,
and the only thing i know for certain
is that every one of them ends in
"why."
tomorrows seem
to come in abundance now
even if they're dressed like
yesterdays. maybe one of these
days, i'll get it right, figure out
why i can't stop self-destructing,
because there is always going to be
another tomorrow, another chance
to disconnect the ticking bomb inside
of me—at least, until there isn't.

binge

i lapsed yesterday. well, technically it started the night before, but yesterday was the worst of it—and i don't mean the worst of the two days, or the worst in recent memory, but the worst episode of bingeing i've ever had in my entire life. i've slipped up before this, but i could at least blame those instances on the whiskey. this was all me—or whatever it is inside of me i have yet to tame. think black hole but don't actually think blackhole because i've exhausted that metaphor more times than i care to count. i don't think blackholes feel shame, anyway. or how painful it is to breathe when your stomach is lined with a thousand little knives that make every inhalation feel like a death sentence. in some ways, it *is* a death sentence. not for me, or my "progress," but for the delusion that i ever had any of this under my control.

I FEEL LIKE I'M SPIRALING
AND FOR ONCE,
I WANT THE SPINNING TO
STOP.

repetition

i begin my morning
and end my night
the very same way:
in front of the bathroom mirror
tearing myself apart.
i tilt my head in every direction
and pick out every flaw.
i pull up my shirt and take
in both front and side
views of my body.
i press my hand against my stomach
like i'm tamping down
espresso grounds
and guesstimate how many more pounds
i need to lose before i finally feel worthy
of my reflection,
how many more calories i need to cut
to burn the masculinity from my bones.
but my reflection
isn't the villain here,
nor is it my body—
it's me,
for ever allowing myself
to be degraded
the way i degrade myself
every single day.

what is 2021 if not 2019 persevering?

i've gained 35 pounds
of guilt over the last year
for the way 2020 felt
like it was going to be "mine."
for using the lockdown
to lock me inside myself
until my headspace
was a better place.
i tried trading whiskey for kombucha,
binge eating for diet and exercise,
overthinking for mindfulness.
i made a point to get healthier
despite the world getting sicker.
but here i am at the cusp of the new year,
and it feels a lot like 2019 in that i've slid
back down the hole i all but dragged
myself out of, and all i can do is watch
helplessly as rock bottom
welcomes me back
with its mouth wide open
as if to say, "i'll always
be here for you, especially
when you aren't there
for yourself."

THERE IS AN EMPTINESS INSIDE
I CANNOT EXPLAIN—
A LONGING FOR SOMETHING
I CANNOT GIVE A NAME.

hate

i hate waking up
and i hate going to bed.
i hate deciding what to eat
and i hate cooking it.
i even hate eating sometimes.
i hate brushing my teeth
and showering,
and the way my hair
falls out when i wash it.
i hate doing laundry
and washing dishes by hand.
but i also hate unloading the dishwasher,
and putting things back where they belong.
i hate picking an outfit for the day
because i hate how everything fits.
i hate going grocery shopping
because i hate the crowds
and i hate being perceived.
i hate how often i have to take a piss,
and how i can't go into a public
restroom without fearing violence.
i hate this poem and the way i'm rambling
and i hate the way my brain operates.
i hate how every day is the same
as yesterday and i hate when
tomorrow is different than today.

writer's block

the cursor blinks uninterrupted for nearly
twenty minutes and it feels like it's
taunting me, daring me to do something
just because it knows i won't.
but i do. i type, and type and type

and i look at something that is shaped
like a poem, but there is no poetry in it—
just the ramblings of someone who can
never find a word big enough to hold their
feelings. so i delete and delete and delete

and wish i was writing on paper because then
at least there would be a crumpled-up ball
to show for it. i settle for crumpling myself up
on the floor. i unfold myself in between the pages
of a poetry book and think about how everyone

is so much better at this than me. if comparison
is the thief of joy then it's no wonder i hate
everything i've ever written. i put the book down,
question if i've ever had a single original thought
in my life, ask myself why i even bother writing

them down when someone else has already
articulated it a million times more beautifully,
and then i try to convince myself that there is
at least one person out there who needs *my*
version of it, even if that person is just myself.

do as i say not as i do

i'm so good at giving advice
but so bad at taking my own.
here's a platitude for you to drink in,
to sip and swirl around in your mouth
until the truth ignites your tongue.
none for me, though—i'm already
drunk enough on my own bullshit.

breakup poem

i think it's time we go
our own separate ways.
i swear it's not you, it's me.
the past five years have
been great—you've helped
me discover so much
about myself—but i don't
think i have anything left
to give. i've said everything
i needed to say, and to
keep writing these poems
means to risk overstaying
my welcome. i'm not strong
enough to endure another
failure, so maybe it's best
to take the little bit of success
i've garnered and let this
coffee-and-whiskey-stained
chapter of my life
be our ending.

IS THE POET
STILL A POET
WHEN THEIR PEN
HAS RUN DRY?

i dream about a version of me that still has friends

this version of me sits on the floor of a cramped, dimly lit living room where everyone talks and laughs and passes a large pizza box around until everybody has a slice. this version of me doesn't stumble over her words or struggle to come up with interesting things to say. this version of me doesn't wonder if people are perceiving her the way she deserves to be seen or if they're just entertaining her. this version of me has a green thumb for tending to relationships, and in turn, is filled with life by them. the real version of me that can't even keep an air plant alive, wakes up 9 minutes before her alarm, a hollow in her heart, wishing she could've slept for just a few minutes more.

social distance—

it's something i'm somewhat of an expert on.
i go months without talking to family,
years without talking to my old friends,
and it's as natural to me as breathing.
i scroll through instagram and window shop
for relationships i know i lack the emotional
currency to tend to. and yet, green
is in abundance when i watch connections
between others intertwine and blossom
into rolling fields of sunshine roses.
dead soil can only grow other dead things,
and i'm tired of being a graveyard.

dysphoria iii

i mourn a version
of myself
that never got to be
every time
i see a woman
drink from a cup
of femininity
i will never get to taste.

"my battery is low and it's getting dark"

how many more times do i need to wake up plastered
against the hardwood floor to realize the next stop is
six feet deep? how many more times can i tell myself,
"i have this under control" while i'm spiraling out of it?
the blackout swallows me whole, while my memory has
more holes in it than the tray of bagel bites i accidentally
left in the oven to burn a few years back that i only know
about because my wife found me passed out in front of it.
who would've thought that this "straight edge" teenager
would become the type of person to get shitfaced in front
of all their peers at dinner, slam a martini glass down
like thor demanding another, and shatter their self-
respect in the palm of their hand? this isn't who she wanted
to become when she grew up, so add my name to the list
of people i've let down. i just hope my battery lasts long
enough to keep the darkness at bay until i find redemption.

always becoming, never being

i'm like a cocooned caterpillar caught in the middle of its metamorphosis, wings in waiting, dreaming of being, of finally taking flight under starlight, icarus in reverse—running from sunlight, chasing moonlight.

I KNOW I THRIVE AT NIGHT
BUT I HAVEN'T YET GIVEN UP
ON MY LIGHT.

this isn't even my final form

i'm a master class in shape-shifting in that no two photos of me ever really look the same, and self-love sometimes comes in the form of scrolling through my camera roll and finding the common thread that connects every single one of them. it's not about how i look or what's happening in the moment, but rather looking for where you can see the real me breaking through. it's noticing where i had the courage to discard normalcy for authenticity in even the smallest bits. it's looking for that spark of confidence, no matter how dimly it may be glowing. it's watching that spark become a flame become a star become a galaxy with every passing year. it's realizing that i am the most me i've ever been in this very moment. and tomorrow, i will be the most me i've ever been in that moment. and ten years from now, i will be the most me i've ever been in that moment. and when my body is ash and my soul is stardust, i will be the most me i've ever been.

the woman in the moon

after Joshua Jennifer Espinoza

i've been too much in my own head, these days.
how can i not be when it's the only place to go?
i thought i had figured myself out already—
left old versions of myself behind, stepped out
of the dark and let the sunlight kiss my skin, etc.,
found an identity and draped myself in yellow,
white, purple, and black stripes—but out here,
where the world is as still as the bone-cold air, where
the moon wears a full face and glows in all her glory
against the vastness of the universe, i feel her pull
me in like she does every time i catch a glimpse
of her in any of her phases, and every time i meet
her gaze, i feel like i'm looking into a mirror.
there's always a moment where every thought
darts across my mind like shooting stars, hoping
to be the one i catch and dwell on, but this time,
there is a certain quietness i'm not used to, one
that's interrupted when i think i hear a woman
call out to me using a name that isn't mine but feels
like maybe it should be. i ask her who she is and she
tells me that i already know. she tells me that she's
been screaming for twenty-something years waiting
for me to hear her, and that she will not be ignored
for a second longer. i tell her i'm sorry. i tell her
i hear her. i tell her that i'm finally ready to listen.

dawn

i've been making it a habit to leave
the blinds cracked open when i go
to bed. i've realized i've taken sunlight
and blue skies for granted, so i'm taking
in as many clear days as i can.

SUNRISE

lake michigan

i write a lot about finding myself for someone who never really seems to do it. i have seen lakes that look like oceans and if i didn't know better, you could convince me that one was the other and i'd be none the wiser. i don't know what the end of this search looks like, but i want to believe i'm close. i want to believe i'll know the difference when i see it.

december 10th, 2020

despite it all, 2020 was a catalyst for so much change
it's like i've become an entirely different person.
i've decided to leave the old versions of me behind,
and i'm leaving my birth name behind along with them.

name change: granted

the thing about naming your child after yourself is that you never anticipate what a dick you might become, and how much your kid will grow up to resent you for it. you gifted me this name not knowing it was a curse, and when i was old enough to think for myself, i took a knife to it and cut it in half to make it a little easier to swallow. your name never fit me for so many reasons, and if i'm being honest, severing the connection with you wasn't even the most important one, but now when i look at my name, when i write it down, when i say it out loud, and when i hear it from her mouth, it doesn't sound like a haunted house, but like the windchimes hanging outside of our home when they sing in the late october breeze. this was the last grip you held on me after being absent for nearly a decade, and now i am completely and utterly
f r e e .

SAY GOODBYE TO WHO YOU WERE
TO MAKE SPACE FOR WHO YOU ARE
MEANT TO BE.

you have new memories to look back on today

new birthdays!
deadname tags
old family photos
photos of a me
that no longer
exists
out-of-date jokes
i used to find
funny
2016
politics
our wedding day
casual
transphobia
from friends
who aren't
friends
anymore
reminders
of how
quickly
and completely
life can
change—
for better
or for worse

when the poems are closets

i write a poem about a teenager questioning
their own reflection in a mirror, but leave out
the part where the gender they were assigned at birth
is the reason for the discomfort they're growing into.

i write a poem about whiskey being the catalyst
for my truth to be spoken for the first time, but leave out
the part where what i drunkenly blurt out to my partner
is that i wished i was a woman.

i write a poem about how one day, i will not have to hide
my pride in the back of a closet, but leave out
the part where i literally tuck my pride flag into the back
of a closet as i welcome guests into my home.

i write poem after poem about being transgender,
but always leave out the fact that i *am* transgender,
making my words just vague enough, just
palatable enough that anyone can relate.

the poems become the same closet that my pride flag
once lay folded neatly inside, the same place
in the back of my mind where that teen tucked away
their gender dysphoria before it had a name.

the poems that were meant to set me free become
one more place to lock myself away, but now,
i'm making up for it by ripping all the closet doors
off their hinges so there's no place left to hide,

and even when my sunset comes and i drift to sleep
for the very last time, there will be no casket to close,
no grave to bury me in, because who i am cannot be
contained by anything less than the universe herself.

I AM IN LOVE WITH THE
POSSIBILITY OF THE PERSON
I MIGHT SOMEDAY BECOME.

hey siri, play "all i have to give the world is me" by tegan and sara

it's 7:36 in the morning and the new york city skyline
is the fiery reflection of the sun rising over the atlantic.
in less than 20 minutes, i will spend the next 7 hours
being called "mister" while i masquerade as a cis man,
but for the next 2 minutes and 54 seconds, i am me,
just me, driving the winding backroad to my job,
belting out the chorus of my favorite song with tears
stinging my eyes as i practice keeping my larynx
raised as high as the empire state building.
for the next 2 minutes and 54 seconds, i wonder
what would happen if i gave the whole world
the whole me, *just me, and that's it.*

expectations

my wife does an oracle card reading for the collective
on instagram, and i know deep down the trans goddesses
were conspiring with her to deliver this message directly
to me, specifically. the caption reads: "you don't need to be
the person others expect you to be. be who YOU are,"
and suddenly i'm that teenager standing in front of the mirror
again, but this time, i understand everything. i understand
that locking myself away in a mental closet is not sustainable.
and i understand for the first time that if i am not being
honest with myself, then i am not being honest with anybody.

SHE TELLS ME SHE SUPPORTS ME
AND I THINK THAT IS A POEM IN ITSELF.

june 5th, 2021

it's 8:00 pm and it's time for my very first dose.
i take a little light blue tablet and place it beneath
my tongue. it takes about 15 minutes for it
to fully dissolve, but the emotions are instantaneous.
i have fought arriving at this moment
with every fiber of my being for so very long
that the moment i rest my tongue on top
of the tablet, a mixture of relief and disbelief.
disbelief because i never saw this future for me,
relief because i am finally becoming who i
was always meant to be.

"are you a boy? or are you a girl?"

when professor oak first asked me that question
back in 2001, there wasn't a doubt in my mind.
at least, not one i could conceivably understand
as a thirteen-year-old kid from the midwest.
i clicked "boy" because "boy" is all i knew
how to be, and i continued clicking "boy"
out of habit until well after i realized i wasn't one.
one time, i chose "girl" just to see if it felt
any more right than clicking "boy,"
and it didn't feel wrong, but nostalgia
and comfort prevented it from feeling right.
one time, i changed my sims character
from man to woman, watched the boxy edges
soften into curves, and watched the polygonal
version of myself become who she should've
been from the moment she was created,
and i wondered how different my life would be
if it were that easy—a simple question,
a gender toggle. if you would've asked
me at birth, at the hormonal crossroads
of puberty: "are you a boy? or are you a girl?"
i would've chosen "girl" every single time.

the only time i call myself "she" is in my poetry

it's easier when i remove myself from it, pretend who i'm writing about isn't me, or at least some distant version of me who's had a little more time to grow into herself. maybe if i write it down enough times, i'll start believing it.

existential

i want to live so much more life than we're allowed to and i don't know how to cope with it. there are nights where i stare up at the stars, look at my reflection in the moon, let the cool air chill me to my soul, and am burdened with how small i am compared to the universe even though it's no small miracle that i am here. i am burdened with how society has siphoned away the miraculousness of it all by replacing the sun as the center of our solar system with the dollar bill. just as the universe is endlessly expanding beyond itself, i, too, have outgrown myself. i have outgrown homes and cities and states. i have outgrown a country, a society, a world that would rather see me dead than let me *simply be.* and though i haven't outgrown the universe, i am certainly catching up to her.

YOU ARE MEANT FOR MORE THAN JUST SURVIVING.
YOU ARE MEANT FOR MORE THAN JUST SURVIVING.
YOU ARE MEANT FOR MORE THAN JUST SURVIVING.
YOU ARE MEANT FOR MORE THAN JUST SURVIVING.
YOU ARE MEANT FOR MORE THAN JUST SURVIVING.
YOU ARE MEANT FOR MORE THAN JUST SURVIVING.
YOU ARE MEANT FOR MORE THAN JUST SURVIVING.
YOU ARE MEANT FOR MORE THAN JUST SURVIVING.
YOU ARE MEANT FOR MORE THAN JUST SURVIVING.
YOU ARE MEANT FOR MORE THAN JUST SURVIVING.
YOU ARE MEANT FOR MORE THAN JUST SURVIVING.
YOU ARE MEANT FOR MORE THAN JUST SURVIVING.
YOU ARE MEANT FOR MORE THAN JUST SURVIVING.
YOU ARE MEANT FOR MORE THAN JUST SURVIVING.
YOU ARE MEANT FOR MORE THAN JUST SURVIVING.
YOU ARE MEANT FOR MORE THAN JUST SURVIVING.
YOU ARE MEANT FOR MORE THAN JUST SURVIVING.
YOU ARE MEANT FOR MORE THAN JUST SURVIVING.
YOU ARE MEANT FOR MORE THAN JUST SURVIVING.
YOU ARE MEANT FOR MORE THAN JUST SURVIVING.
YOU ARE MEANT FOR MORE THAN JUST SURVIVING.

screaming insecurities

imposter syndrome never really goes away,
a constant crisis that comes and goes just
to make us question our place in the world.
what *does* belonging look like? is it a state of
being accepted or just a state of being? i write,
but sometimes it doesn't feel like i belong
on the same shelf as other writers, let alone
the same book. i've been on hormones for 11 months,
4 days, and 2 hours but sometimes i feel like
i'm not trans enough. it's like always looking
through a window and never being on the other
side of it, even though you know you belong,
even though your existence alone is enough
to break glass ceilings and shatter expectations.

see me.

don't just look at me.
push away any preconceptions
you have of me, the notion
that you know me better
than i know myself.

see me.
not just in shades
of black and white,
but in the baby blues and pinks
i now drape myself in.

see me.
not who you knew
once upon a time,
but the person that lives
and breathes here and now.

see me.
for the glitter glistening
on my eyelids,
and the stardust
shining in my soul.

whether you acknowledge it or not,
whether you accept it or not,
i am who i am, and i am
so proud to finally
be able to say that.

YOU PRETENDING NOT TO SEE
DOESN'T MAKE IT CEASE TO BE.

spotted lanternfly

they tell us if we see 'em, kill 'em
on sight. stomp 'em, suck 'em up
with starbucks cups and freeze 'em
until their freckled flames flicker
and die. they say they're invasive,
that they destroy the ecosystem,
but all i hear is that at any point
in time, we can decide that an entire
species is not worthy of its life,
even when we don't fully understand it.

conservative ~~values~~ hypocrisy

they say

ban
books
ban
tiktok
ban
drag queens
ban
marriage equality
ban
abortion
ban
birth control
ban
pronouns
ban
chosen names
ban
gender-affirming care
ban
trans people from sports
ban
trans people from bathrooms
ban
trans people
ban
diversity
ban
inclusivity
ban

sex ed
ban
gender studies
ban
Black history
ban
american history
ban
critical race theory
ban
critical thinking

in the name of
protecting children

but they won't say

ban
assault weapons

'cause "bans
don't work."

everything is fake

the earth is spinning faster
and time—the ultimate construct—
is up for debate. if 1.59 milliseconds
can upend how an entire society defines
what constitutes a day, then how
can one ever argue that gender
is some sort of universal truth?

EYESHADOW WAS MY SHIELD.
LIPSTICK IS MY SWORD.

let kids be kids

when
they say
"let kids be kids"
what they mean is
"let kids *stay* kids
forever" because
they'd rather
have a dead
kid than a
trans kid

eradicate

the year i went on hormones, 144 pieces of anti-trans legislation were introduced in the united states.

the year i came out as a woman, 591 (and counting) pieces of anti-trans legislation were introduced.

they call us "groomers," "mutants," and "imps."

they say we should be "eradicated from public life entirely."

they try to legislate us out of existence by taking away our life-saving medication, banning pronouns and chosen names, making it a crime to simply be trans in the presence of children.

but no matter what laws they pass, no matter the dehumanizing language they use to describe us, we will always be here, queer, and living

unapologetically ourselves.

YOU'RE AFRAID
OF SOMETHING YOU REFUSE
TO UNDERSTAND.
I'M AFRAID
OF WHAT YOU'LL DO
OUT OF THAT IGNORANCE.

just keep rollin'

this boy who merely lived
grew up to be a woman who thrived,
and you can tweet from your castle,
drape yourself in the language
of the oppressor, become nameless
to the very same people who hid
in your words when they needed
an escape. but in this story, like any,
the best part is always when love
triumphs, and hate becomes nothing
more than a footnote in history.
until then, i'll just keep rollin'.

pride 2023

i.

i put on my makeup first—
my usual smokey eye
accented by sharp wings,
bronzer to put some color
onto my ghostly ginger skin,
enough highlighter to stop
a terf in their tracks.
i line my lips and paint them
in my favorite shade,
so long summer, the irony
not lost on me that summer
hasn't even officially begun yet.
then, i slip into my shapewear,
slide on my "support trans futures"
t-shirt and tie it over the waistband
of my black maxi skirt.
i style my hair in low spacebuns and
crown myself with a black sunhat.
in the full-length mirror, i admire
the work two years of hormones
put into helping me embrace
the person looking back at me.
dare i say, she's even pretty cute.

ii.

i pull on my combat boots,
tie their purple laces,
and march with my wife

to the park in the heart of town,
past the cops blocking
the tent-lined streets,
past the picnic tables of people
enjoying the entertainment,
to our very first pride festival.
a group of older townies turn
their attention from the cover
band on stage to look me over
in a way as if to say, “look, it’s one
of them transgenders.” i’ve come
so far with accepting myself
that i sometimes forget that
even at pride, not everyone is
as accepting of who i have become
as i am. i start searching for escape
routes and places to hide,
and settle on taking a seat at
the queerest looking table
with hopes of blending in.

iii.

we get up and briefly check
out pride flag adorned vendors,
take selfies to celebrate
ourselves and our queerness,
get cupcakes and sparkling
water, and then make our escape.
as we turn the corner, a man
in a midlife-crisis-mobile
barks “jesus christ” loud enough
to cut through the humming of
a dozen car engines lined up at

the intersection, and i don't know
if he's cursing me or the traffic,
but instantly i am a teen again, walking
home from the mall, getting called
a "faggot" by the cars speeding by.
the difference is, i didn't understand
myself back then the way i do now,
so teen me brushes it off, while
present day me fights back the sting
of tears the whole way home, grateful
for the protection of big sunglasses.

iv.

i find myself back in front of the mirror,
knowing i had one more place to go to,
contemplating makeup wipes
and an outfit change. i once again
come face to face with my reflection
but this time, struggle to meet her
twinkling, tear-filled eyes, and i think
about the closet she had to scratch and claw
her way out of, about how she spent years
talking herself out of being who she is.
so for her, i choke down my fear, brush
the tears from my cheeks, and put the
makeup wipes back in the cabinet.
for her, i decide that hate does not get to win.
hate does not get to shove me back into that closet.
hate does not get to talk me out of being myself.
i decide that today, tomorrow, and every day after,

trans joy wins.

STARDUST

transmute

i am no god but i can perform miracles just as well.

watch as i turn whiskey into water—forgiving
the killing thing for its sins and making it holy.

watch as i turn a casket into a home—cleansing
from it the stench of death by filling it with life.

watch as i turn a human into a wonder—reclaiming
this leaden body and transforming it into something golden.

watch as i die and come back to life—resurrecting
into the person i was always meant to be.

regular

i decided to become a ghost at my old haunts.
out of sight, out of mind, as they like to say.
if i disappeared long enough, perhaps they'd
forget my old name/my old face. i started driving
the opposite way down the coastline to another
coffee shop, one where the baristas never knew
who i used to be. and it was easy. too easy.
but that's the thing—the easy path is rarely the
most rewarding one. and it wasn't until i
came back to *my* coffee shop, and heard *my*
favorite barista call *my* name, that i had
finally realized what i was missing out on.

dead names stay dead

i hate confrontation, which means i let a lot of shit slide. while keeping the peace at the expense of myself is not something i'm unfamiliar with, there comes a point where peace isn't enough, where people-pleasing becomes less like putting out a fire and more like throwing gasoline on top of it, and my patience has grown wick-thin. it's been over three years since i burned my dead name to ashes and let them blow away with the last chilly wind as winter transitioned into spring. i understand more than anyone that change can only come with time, but time isn't some magical entity that does all the work for you—an effort still needs to be made. you can plant seeds in the newly warmed soil, but unless you water them and nourish them, they may never fully blossom. to speak my name to my face, to tell me you support me no matter what, while keeping my dead name alive and well when you think i can't hear it being uttered, is not that effort, and it's not supportive—it's barren ground that will never sustain anything meaningful, and i will not be made to feel responsible for the death of anything someone chooses to plant there.

text me when ur sober

i'm getting drunk on early mornings.
waking up with the sun, watching her
rise over the atlantic and paint the sky
in every single color—even the ones
i can't see. a warm mug of coffee in one
hand as i pet our cats with the other.
quiet wrapped around me like a cardigan.
there is a certain stillness that exists only
in these moments, a stillness thrumming
with energy, with possibility, with life,
and it's so damn intoxicating in a way
that whiskey-fueled nights can never be.

MAKE ME GOLDEN LIKE AN AUTUMN SUNRISE.

"we are the jack-o'-lanterns in july"

i hate the summer, but
you help me find the magic in it—

pumpkin spice coffee in the morning
before pumpkin spice season has even begun.

iced lattes and early-afternoon drives while
singing fall out boy lyrics at the top of our lungs
through the tree-lined county roads.

two scoops of ice cream at the marina
while the sun paints us with golden strokes.

wandering through fields of sunflowers
in search of the one that shines the brightest
(even though all their faces turn to follow yours).

picking our own peaches and looking up
the different desserts we can make with them.

it's not quite autumn, but it doesn't have to be
when you and i are october personified.

safe space

before the poetry, there were two young adults who saw something about themselves in each other. there were two young adults who bonded through sarcasm and over heartbreak. there were two young adults who called each other their twin because they were so alike in so many ways. there were two young adults who were willing to kill the 650 miles between them to get to each other. 10 years later, and they are as in sync with each other as ever. and they feel safe enough to be entirely themselves around one another, but also safe enough to journey within themselves and practice the messy yet beautiful art of becoming. safe enough to continue becoming, even if it takes them to places they never thought they'd go, because they know the other will be waiting for them at the end, ready to take them by the hand and make the journey back home together.

FOREVER GROWING INTO OURSELVES.
FOREVER GROWING INTO EACH OTHER.

where you lead, i will follow

take me to the forest
where a chilly breeze is always blowin'
and the leaves stay forever golden

take me to the city
where the days are never the same
and nobody remembers our names

take me to the coast
where the trees line the bay
and the tide never sweeps us away

take me to the café
where the coffee is endlessly abrew
and there's always a table for two

take me to the bookstore
where poetry is the only category
and every shelf chronicles our story

take me to the cove
where the cats are always at play
and with me you'll forever stay

she says she's not a perfect partner

after amanda lovelace

but she fully supports me when i tell her i want to transition.

she updates my pronouns in all of her old poetry books.

she goes with me into public restrooms to make sure i am safe.

she holds up my hair and puts ointment on my gender affirming surgery scar.

she introduces me to others as her wife without any hesitation.

she never treats me any different, no matter how much i change.

she stays. she stays. she stays.

don't wanna live, don't wanna die

we lay in bed beside each other,
and one second, we're laughing
between coughs and the next,
i'm crying. i'm crying and i don't
know how to tell you that i'm scared.
i don't know how to tell you that
i'm scared because nearly 7 million
people have died from this sickness
and even though we've survived
for 3 years, i'm terrified
that our luck has run out.
i'm terrified of what happens if one
of us doesn't wake up tomorrow,
how the other will cope.
i think about sneaking out of bed
and writing my final wishes
"just in case," but i can't bring myself
to face my mortality in the reflection
of the computer screen.
i joked to you one night before bed
that i don't wanna live
but i don't want to die
and what i meant was that
existence is an exhausting thing—
it's hard, and it's ugly, and it hurts,
but it's also fragile, magical, and beautiful,
and the fear of leaving you behind
or worse, losing you, is infinitely
more frightening than anything
that has made me so apathetic to living.
when i awake the next morning

i pause. i listen for your breath,
i look for the rise and fall of your chest.
i let out a sigh of relief knowing
our tomorrows haven't yet run out.
it is a part of my morning ritual now.
before brushing my teeth,
before the first sip of coffee,
i allow myself to be grateful
that we are here, breathing,
because that's all that really matters.

lavender haze

for yule, she gifts me a fancy new espresso machine and enough accessories to make a professional barista envious, and while i'm far from a pro, i'm just as passionate about the craft as one. all these years later and coffee is as big a part of our relationship as ever—from the very first cup they brewed me in a mr. coffee one fateful october afternoon in 2012, all the way to me teaching them how to make the perfect pour-over—and every single carryout cup in between—the scent of coffee is always lingering around us. lattes become our new morning ritual: freshly roasted beans from our favorite coffee shop, steamed oat milk, two pumps of lavender and two pumps of hazelnut syrups—the lavender haze, we've named it. sometimes there's a milk-foam heart in the mug i hand her, other times there's only the sign that an attempt was made, but there's never a lack of my own heart in it, because this? this is our love language—coffee, together, whenever, wherever we may be.

SHE IS MY OCTOBER SOULMATE,
MY LAVENDER LOVE.

one year sober

i am not one to separate the different versions of myself into their own person, but just this once, i think i'll make an exception—an exception for the version i left behind a year ago. the person who'd let "one more glass" become three more swigs directly from the neck of the bottle. the one who thought they knew when enough was enough, only to end up blacked out on the hardwood floor. i know that version of me is like a lingering aftertaste on the tongues of so many people who had the misfortune of meeting them first, a taste that may never go away, but as for me? i've poured the last of that person down the drain, i've ripped the fairy lights out of the empty bottles above the kitchen cabinets and tossed the reminders in the recycling bin. i've purged that person from my system once and for all, and i am refusing to let myself be defined by them for even a second longer.

manhattan

i used to use every trip to the city as an excuse to go on a day-long drinking binge. i think of one in particular—it was a cool august evening and i was already three manhattans deep. after dinner, we headed out to the terrace of the hotel room and i stayed up until the early morning hours drinking spiked arnold palmers and a half-pint of irish whiskey straight from the neck of the bottle. everything around me had this muddied quality to it, like nothing else existed outside of myself, like i barely existed within myself. i know i enjoyed the company of family, i know the 8th floor felt like the top of the empire state building, and that i felt untouchable, but i can't remember much else.

here i am, nearly five years later, celebrating over a year of sobriety, and i'm sitting on a terrace on the same exact floor of the same exact hotel, drinking sparkling water and eating doritos, and everything is as crystal clear as my drink—the twinkling skyscrapers, the constant hum of traffic and car horns, the slightly chilly air that makes me wax autumnal, the handful of stars shining just brightly enough to cut through the light pollution, the sight of my wife on the other side of the floor-to-ceiling windows, sitting on the bed, laughing as we send texts back and forth, and the realization that i am no longer living for just the night, but for the sun that rises tomorrow, and every single sunrise after that.

purple aster

now i live with my inner child in mind and for the girl that never knew she could be. i'm teaching her the strength in being soft. i'm dressing her in long flowy dresses and i'm placing a crown of autumn leaves and purple asters in her hair, one that matches every color of her october soul. i'm painting her lips in a delicate pink just so she knows she can—even if she'll always prefer a bold black. i'm letting her know she can eat a bagel and cream cheese every single morning if she wants to—calories be damned—and that the number on the scale is just that—a number. i'm giving her the ability to love what she sees in the mirror, especially when it isn't easy, because that's when she'll need to the most. i'm showing her how to be gentle with her own heart, so she doesn't let anyone take it for granted, and so she knows how to show the love-of-her-life's heart that same gentleness.

THEY'RE WRITING "SHE" POEMS.
I'M BECOMING THE "SHE" IN HERS.

queer love

her lipstick in my desk.
my lipstick on her carryout cup.

my curls in between her fingers.
her hair tie around my wrist.

lavender oat milk lattes.
matching plaid outfits.

selfies for no reason.
selfies for every reason.

"i'm a lesbian," she says.
"i'm a woman," i say.

two haircut and gel manicure appointments.
flowers. oh, so many flowers.

driving through our conservative town,
windows down, chappell roan on full blast.

retaking our wedding photos
(but make it sapphic).

finally changing my social media bios
from "spouse of" to "wife of."

gender marker

it's a gloomy, early morning,
but she still wakes up to go with me.
we stop at a drive-through for coffee
and head to the dmv with my 6 points
of identification and a gender marker
declaration form tucked into an envelope.
the last time i was here, i had x'd out
the gender i was assigned at birth from
my driver's license, but i hadn't known
myself then the way i do now. two years
is but a few specks in the sands of time,
and yet it's long enough to change your
entire perception of who you really are.
i feel like all i've done lately is change,
but i know deep down that's not true.
i haven't changed at all—i've just gotten
to really know myself for the first time
in my entire life. this time, i mark "f"
on my application, i hand over my proof-
of-identity, my gender marker declaration
form, and my current driver's license.
i get the ugliest photo of me ever taken
(a rite of passage, perhaps), pay the eleven
dollar processing fee, and get my new
temp license. i meet back up with my wife
and she walks with me into the women's
restroom where i pee for the first time
as a legally-recognized woman.

THERE IS NOTHING
MORE DELICATE
IN THE UNIVERSE
THAN A LOVE
BETWEEN TWO WOMEN.

like mother

i'm seeing my father's face in the mirror less and less these days, and more of my mother's. it's something i didn't expect when i started transitioning two and a half years ago, and maybe it's only subtle enough for me to notice, but it has to be something of a gift. i think about how my father doesn't have any idea of the person i have become, who might not even know that i disowned his name back in 2020 the same way he disowned his family, and i compare it to the way my mother, who, even from another state, has witnessed me become who i wish i'd been brave enough to be as a kid, my mother who this year sent me a birthday card that read "my daughter is amazing" when she could've pretended not to see the version of myself that my father will never know. now when i look at myself in pictures, or catch my reflection from the right angle, i am grateful that it isn't the parent that walked away that i am reminded of anymore, but the one who never stopped giving her love and support unconditionally.

some kind of magic

she teaches me the art of releasing on the full moon
and how to find the mystical in the simple and mundane.

they teach me how to manifest my dreams
and what candle colors and crystals contain which properties.

she teaches me how to enchant my coffee
and how to interpret what my tarot cards are telling me.

they teach me the magic of loving myself
and how that is the most important spell of them all.

"what is a woman?"

when they say putting on a dress and wearing makeup
doesn't make you a woman, i agree with them. for me,

it's the way the child version of myself shared a much deeper friendship with the girl that lived next door than she did with her brother.

it's the way the teenage version of myself always felt like she was "one of the girls" in her aol chat group, and never really connected with any of the boys.

it's the way the young adult version of myself felt like she "wasn't like other guys," before realizing that maybe she wasn't one at all.

it's the way the adult version of myself felt like she loved women "in a gay way" even though she didn't understand how that could possibly be.

it's the way the current version of myself was always told where her place was and never given the chance to bloom because society had different expectations for her.

it's the way that no matter how i try to explain how i know i am a woman, there aren't any words to explain it, because the answer only exists in how the universe conspired to create me.

so when they ask "what is a woman?" tell them
"motherfucking stardust."

YOU ARE SO MUCH MORE
THAN THEY COULD EVER COMPREHEND.

serotonin

i've started seeing a therapist regularly and taking medication to treat my anxiety and depression. it's only been a few weeks, but i'm hanging on to the hope that this will all make a difference. i think this is self-care, because i don't know that i would've reached out for help if i didn't start loving myself along the way.

one is all, all is one

i hold the weight of the moon in one palm, and the sun in the other. i sprinkle stardust over my eyelids and root my feet deep into the earth. it's a balancing act, you see. here, there is harmony. here, there is peace. not always, of course, but it now exists where it didn't before, and i am hanging on to it with all the life the universe has gifted me with.

forget-me-nots

i am as much the same as i am different.

i'm still the kid who gets excited every time a new sonic or pokémon game comes out, who buys trading cards and collectibles of her favorite characters and displays them on her bookshelves. the same kid who is afraid of spiders and centipedes and every single sound she hears when she struggles to fall asleep at night.

i'm still the teenager who knows every lyric to every evanescence song and the exact moment in "conversations" her old finger eleven cd used to skip. the same teenager who loved to dress in black clothes and smudged black makeup around her eyes because it made her feel more at home in her body.

i'm still the young adult who puts too much sweet'n low in her morning coffee and opens a can of the blue rockstar energy drink to be reminded of the carefree midwestern summers traveling down i-94. the same young adult who loves so much more than she ever knows how to put into words, who dreams of the moon, the night sky, and swimming in oceans of stardust.

i'm still the same me, no matter how much i've grown, and i'll never forget who i've been as i've perfected the art of becoming.

WHAT MADE YOU SO AFRAID
TO BE YOURSELF?

hrt is alchemy

i start by dissolving a little blue pill
underneath my tongue twice a day,
then three times a day, before switching

to weekly injections. it feels a little like a ritual,
a little like magic, like i'm placing an offering
on the altar of a goddess i worship, except the goddess

is me and i am her because i pray to no man,
no storybook savior. if you want something done right,
you must do it yourself, so i draw 0.3 milliliters

of the elixir of life into a syringe and i plunge
it into my body, i swallow the sun and the moon,
i watch myself become golden, perfected,

and i realize that this right here is my magnum
opus. not a poem, not a masterpiece, not my body
of work, but me.

i am the poem.
i am the masterpiece.
i am my greatest work.

call me hot, not pretty

i paint my lips a spicy red, pack
shimmery purple pigment around
my eyes and put on my good bra—
the one that gives me a little cleavage.
i slip into a low-cut black maxi dress,
cinching my waist with a corset belt
to highlight the slightest hourglass
shape hiding beneath the loose cloth.
i think to myself, "damn, she's hot."
i've always been too ashamed of this
body to ever feel myself like this,
but now i embrace these moments,
no matter how fleeting they may be.
sometimes, i'll document it by taking
a few pictures to post on instagram.
sometimes, i'll document it by taking
pictures that no one else is ever gonna
see so i can admire all the ways my
body has transformed: the softness
of my skin, the new curves of my
hips, the starbursts of stretch marks
on my chest, all of it the tangible proof
of just how much i've grown into myself,
because this body i used to hate
is now something to be marveled at.

YOU SAY YOU WANT TO MAKE ART
BUT YOU ARE ALREADY A MASTERPIECE.

remington noiseless

the typewriter on my bookshelf can barely get out a single line of text before it gets stuck and types over itself in an inky mess, and i've related to that for too long. i thought i was done with poetry, but this machine was made to write, and so was i—i think we both just needed a little work to rediscover our voices.

on titling my poetry

i used to title every single poem i wrote
until i stopped titling a single one of them.
a title signifies wholeness. completion.
and there is an entire period of my life where
all i did was contemplate the weight of finality
because i feared the end was waiting for me
at the bottom of the next bottle,
at the end of the next binge/restrict cycle,
a casualty of the seemingly never-ending
war between myself and my reflection.
maybe if i left my poems unfinished,
i'd have no choice but to live long enough
to give them their own happily ever after.
or maybe i was just too afraid to close
out that chapter of my life in case i found
myself in another downward spiral
because then i'd become a failure on top
of everything else. but i'm done
looking at life as something to fear.
i'm titling my poems again.
i'm giving the old ones their closure,
and i'm moving on to a clean new page
because i'm not ending this story on a

cliffhanger.

REPLACE MY BLOOD WITH INK
AND LET ME BECOME THE POEM
I'M ALWAYS TRYING TO WRITE.

cover-up tattoo

i am learning how to embrace my failures.
instead of hiding from them or pretending
they don't exist, i'm collecting all the broken
words and permanent ink stains, and creating
something even more beautiful in their place.

sunset

she asks me if i'm a lesbian and i tell her i don't know if i'm allowed to be one, which is to say that yes, i listen to girl in red, yes, i am a woman who loves women, so yes, technically speaking i am in fact a lesbian, but that i am also afraid of those who knew me before i knew myself and what they'll think. i am afraid of taking up space that i may not be welcome in even though i know i belong. that despite finally accepting and embracing who i was always meant to be, i still worry too much about whether other people accept me the same way. this becomes the moment where i let the sun finally set on internalized self-hatred. this is where i wrap myself in a blanket of starlight—no—*become* starlight, and let myself shine oh, so radiantly. this is where i finally give myself permission to stop and *simply be.*

a letter to my past selves

today i'm saying goodbye to you. i'm saying goodbye to you and it isn't a sad thing, but something to celebrate. not because your existence didn't matter, but because it did.

you mattered. you mattered more than you could have ever thought you did. you went through life without ever truly seeing yourself, without knowing the language to describe how you felt, without knowing that you were never alone in those feelings.

because of that, because you didn't want to be seen, you hid so deeply within yourself that you forgot who you were for a while. but all of this hurt and uncertainty wasn't for nothing because i know who i am now. i know who i am and i'm not afraid to be seen. there are people who love me, and there are some days i even love myself.

things aren't perfect—there is still doubt and uncertainty, and i still fight with my reflection, but i'm winning more battles than i'm losing. i even see myself looking back at me, sometimes. but this isn't about me, this is about you.

today, i'm saying goodbye. today, i'm laying a bouquet of forget-me-nots at the altar of myself. today, i'm thanking you for existing. i'm thanking you for surviving, for carrying such a heavy burden for the last 35 years and bringing me this far.

so far, that i may finally take off the mask i'd hidden behind for so long, and let the sunlight kiss my skin. so i may run until i haven't a breath left, and then take flight. so that i may bathe in moonlight, and paint myself with starlight. so i may become the universe i was always meant to be.

a letter to my future self

i hope you continue to grow and stay true to who you are. i hope you never feel like you have to stop being yourself to make anyone else happy. i hope you continue to set boundaries and do anything and everything to protect your peace. i hope that when you look in the mirror, you see *yourself* staring back at you, every single time. i hope when you look at the moon, you know she is looking for your face in her midnight sky. i hope that every time you reach up to the universe to paint your name with starlight, you know that the stars are writing poetry in your honor. i hope you never go a second without knowing that your existence is no small miracle, or that you are loved—so, so loved.

*I AM IN LOVE WITH THE
VERY PERSON I WAS BRAVE
ENOUGH TO BECOME.*

If you, or someone you know, is struggling with mental health, substance abuse, or disordered eating, please know that you are not alone and help is available:

988 Suicide and Crisis Lifeline
Call & Text: 988 (US & Canada)
https://988lifeline.org/
https://988.ca

Trans Lifeline
Call: (877) 565-8860 (US)
(877) 330-6366 (Canada)
https://translifeline.org/

The Trevor Project
Call: 1-866-488-7386 (US)
Text: send START to 678-678 (US)
https://www.thetrevorproject.org/get-help/

Substance Abuse and Mental Health Services Administration (SAMHSA)
Call: 1-800-662-4357 (US)
https://www.samhsa.gov/find-help/national-helpline
Get Help with Substance Abuse (Canada & Provinces/Territories)
https://www.canada.ca/en/health-canada/services/substance-use/get-help-with-substance-use.html

National Eating Disorders Association (NEDA)
Call & Text: (800) 931-2237 (US)
https://www.nationaleatingdisorders.org/

Kids Help Phone (Canada)
Call: 1-800-668-6868
Text: 686868
https://kidshelpphone.ca

notes

The title of the poem on page 17, "what is 2021 if not 2019 persevering?" is a reference to the quote "what is grief, if not love persevering?" from the TV series *Wandavision.*

The poem on page 19, "hate," was inspired by the song "hate" by the band Hawthorne Heights.

The title of the poem on page 27, "my battery is low and it's getting dark," is a quote from a tweet by Jacob Margolis (@JacobMargolis), which is a translation of the last transmission from the Mars rover *Opportunity* before it went dark after surviving 15 years longer than it should have.

The poem on page 30, "this isn't even my final form," is a reference to a meme in which the said line is commonly and mistakenly attributed to the character Frieza from *Dragon Ball Z*. The poem was originally published in the 2024 edition of *The Central Avenue Poetry Prize*, edited by Beau Adler, and published by Central Avenue Poetry. Thank you so much for shortlisting my poem and giving it its first home!

The poem on page 31, "the woman in the moon," was inspired by and is in conversation with the poem "The Moon is Trans" by Joshua Jennifer Espinoza.

The poem on page 43, "hey siri, play 'all i have to give the world is me' by tegan and sara," was inspired by and directly references the song "All I Have to Give the World Is Me" by Tegan and Sara.

The title of the poem on page 47, "'are you a boy? or are you a girl?'" is a quote from the intro to the video game *Pokémon Crystal Version*, where Professor Oak asks the player to choose their gender. Additionally, I'd like thank Instagram user @iamliamreynolds for catching that I got *Pokémon Crystal*'s release year wrong in the initial draft of this poem.

The title of the poem on page 74, "we are the jack-o'-lanterns in july," is a lyric from the Fall Out Boy song "The Phoenix."

The title of the poem on page 77, "where you lead, i will follow," is a reference to the song "Where You Lead" by Carole King, which served as the theme song for the TV show *Gilmore Girls*.

The title of the poem on page 78, "she says she's not a perfect partner," references and is in conversation with a poem by amanda lovelace titled "*what's important is that she feels comfortable enough not to be perfect around them,*" from the book *she followed the moon back to herself.*

The title of the poem on page 99 titled "call me hot, not pretty" is based on a line from "HOT TO GO!" by Chappell Roan, whose music has been super inspiring to me as someone who has finally embraced her identities as both a woman and a lesbian. Thank you for giving this late bloomer a chance to have her own queer girly pop era.

The poem on page 98, "hrt is alchemy," was originally published in the 2025 edition of *The Central Avenue Poetry Prize*, edited by Beau Adler, and published by Central Avenue Poetry. Thank you again for shortlisting another poem and giving it its first home!

acknowledgments

amanda—I don't know who I'd be or where I'd be if not for your endless love and support. I don't think either of us could've possibly imagined what would blossom between us when we met in an AOL chatroom a lifetime ago, or the ways in which we would both grow and change, not just into ourselves, but into each other. Thank you for being my lavender love. I can't wait to continue drinking coffee with you every single day for the rest of our lives.

Summer—Thank you for being only the second person to read this book, for being an amazing hype-woman and human being, and for the years of friendship. Next time we see each other, I owe you a butter pecan iced coffee and a donut!

Alex and Leigh, The Poegeons—Thank you so much for your endless support, the hinged and unhinged group texts, and the Fortnite games. I appreciate y'all more than you know!

Michelle, Beau, Jessica, and Molly and the Central Avenue team—Thank you for believing in my words enough to do another book with me, and for all the work y'all put into making this book what it is today. Working with you is always an honor and a pleasure.

You—If you're reading this, then thank you. Thank you for taking a chance on my poetry, for reading it until the very end, and for being a part of my journey in some way. Without you, there is no "by Parker Lee"—for better or for worse.

Myself—Specifically every past version of myself. Thank you for surviving so that we may finally thrive. I live for every single one of you. <3

about the author

Parker Lee [she/her] is a trans woman poet and storyteller, as well as author of *coffee days whiskey nights* and *espresso shots & forget-me-nots*. A Midwestern transplant, Parker resides in a coastal New Jersey town alongside wife and poetess amanda lovelace (and their three cats), where she can almost always be found not writing when she should be, drinking way too much coffee, and waxing autumnal every single day of the year.

Connect with her on threads, instagram, tiktok, twitch, and substack at @itsparkerlee.

byparkerlee.com